JUL 0 3 2017

Blues

Jared Siemens

LET'S READ
AV²
BY WEIGL™
ADDED VALUE • AUDIO VISUAL

Go to **www.av2books.com**, and enter this book's unique code.

BOOK CODE

Q929575

AV² by Weigl brings you media enhanced books that support active learning.

AV² provides enriched content that supplements and complements this book. Weigl's AV² books strive to create inspired learning and engage young minds in a total learning experience.

Your AV² Media Enhanced books come alive with...

Audio
Listen to sections of the book read aloud.

Video
Watch informative video clips.

Embedded Weblinks
Gain additional information for research.

Try This!
Complete activities and hands-on experiments.

Key Words
Study vocabulary, and complete a matching word activity.

Quizzes
Test your knowledge.

Slide Show
View images and captions, and prepare a presentation.

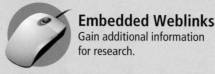

...and much, much more!

Published by AV² by Weigl
350 5th Avenue, 59th Floor
New York, NY 10118
Website: www.av2books.com

Library of Congress Cataloging-in-Publication Data

Siemens, Jared.
  Blues / Jared Siemens.
    pages cm. -- (I love music)
Includes bibliographical references and index.
ISBN 978-1-4896-3573-0 (hard cover : alk. paper) -- ISBN 978-1-4896-3574-7 (soft cover : alk. paper)
ISBN 978-1-4896-3575-4 (single user ebook) -- ISBN 978-1-4896-3576-1 (multi-user ebook)
1. Blues (Music)--History and criticism--Juvenile literature. I. Title.
ML3521.S44 2015
781.64309--dc23
                        2015003073

Printed in the United States of America in Brainerd, Minnesota
1 2 3 4 5 6 7 8 9 0 19 18 17 16 15

072015
170415

Project Coordinator: Jared Siemens
Designer: Mandy Christiansen

The publisher acknowledges Alamy, Getty Images, and iStock as the primary image suppliers for this title.

Blues

CONTENTS

I love music. Blues is my favorite kind of music.

Blues began in the United States during the late 1800s.

5

African Americans from the southern United States made the first blues songs.

Some blues came
from church songs.

Some African Americans sang songs while working. These were the first blues songs.

Singing the blues helps people to remember their stories.

9

A singer's voice is the most important blues instrument. Blues singers stretch out notes so they sound like a cry.

The mood of blues songs is often sad.

Blues songs are often about hard times and hope for a better life.

Blues singers often use words to share their feelings and ideas.

Blues was first played on guitars and banjos.

Some blues artists play the harmonica.

I like to play blues with my friends. Each person plays a different instrument.

I learn to be part of a team when I play blues in a band.

Blues artists play together at festivals. Chicago has the largest free blues festival on Earth.

The Chicago
Blues Festival
began in 1984.

I love blues music. Playing music helps me learn new things.

BLUES FACTS

These pages provide detailed information that expands on the interesting facts found in the book. They are intended to be used by adults as a learning support to help young readers round out their knowledge of each musical genre featured in the *I Love Music* series.

Pages 4–5

I love music. Blues is my favorite kind of music. Music is the name given to sounds made with voices or musical instruments and put together in a way that conveys emotion. People use music to express themselves. Blues is one of the most influential genres in American music history. Blues artists laid the foundation for many modern American musical forms, including jazz, rhythm and blues, rock, and hip-hop.

Pages 6–7

African American people from the southern United States made the first blues songs. Blues began to develop as a genre in the United States near the end of the 19th century. African Americans blended traditional African music with European music to create the blues. African American spirituals were a major influence on the blues. These religious songs often featured themes and imagery from the Christian faith, such as mercy and hope for a new life.

Pages 8–9

Some African Americans sang songs while they worked. African American slaves in early American colonies sang songs in rhythmic time with the tasks they performed. These work songs often used a call and response style. A lead singer would call out a phrase that was then followed by a phrase from other singers. African Americans used blues to help preserve their history from one generation to the next.

Pages 10–11

A singer's voice is the most important blues instrument. Though one or more instruments usually accompany a blues singer, blues is chiefly a vocal genre. Vocalists use a variety of methods to infuse their songs with emotion. Melisma is a vocal technique that involves a singer holding a single syllable while changing notes. Sad-sounding notes, known as blue notes, are also one of the major characteristics of blues.

Blues songs are often about hard times and hope for a better life. The two most common themes in blues lyrics are depression and passion. Blues artists express suffering, loneliness, lost love, and yearning for a better life through their lyrics. While artists in most genres employ narrative lyrics, blues artists focus on lyrics that express their feelings and emotions, rather than lyrics that tell a story.

Blues was first played on guitars and banjos. One of the first blues styles, country blues, was played on acoustic guitar, banjo, or piano. City blues, with its rhythm section, electric guitars, and amplification, developed as African Americans moved from the rural south to northern cities. Blues guitarists can make their instruments "whine" by bending the strings.

I like to play blues with my friends. Playing music with others helps teach children cooperation, teamwork, and how to achieve goals. Children who regularly play music tend to have more confidence and get along better with others. Some students learn better in groups because they do not feel the pressure of having to learn on their own.

Blues artists sometimes play together at festivals. The Chicago Blues Festival began in 1984 to honor Muddy Waters, a legendary blues musician who helped popularize the electric blues. More than half a million blues enthusiasts attend the annual three-day festival to see performances by their favorite artists. Chicago has long been known as the "Blues Capital of the World," due to its rich history of blues music, culture, and local artists.

I love blues music. Playing music helps me learn new things. Recent studies suggest that learning and practicing music can be beneficial to a child's ability to learn. Among these benefits are improved motor skills and dexterity, increased test scores, and even raised Intelligence Quotient, or IQ, scores. Learning music at an early age has also been shown to aid in language development, and to improve reading and listening skills.

KEY WORDS

Research has shown that as much as 65 percent of all written material published in English is made up of 300 words. These 300 words cannot be taught using pictures or learned by sounding them out. They must be recognized by sight. This book contains 59 common sight words to help young readers improve their reading fluency and comprehension. This book also teaches young readers several important content words. These words are paired with pictures to aid in learning and improve understanding.

Page	Sight Words First Appearance	Page	Content Words First Appearance
4	I, is, kind, my, of	4	blues, music
5	began, in, states, the	5	United States
6	American, first, from, made, songs	6	African American
7	came, some	7	church
8	these, were, while	9	stories
9	helps, people, their, to	10	instrument, notes, singer, voice
10	a, important, like, most, out, so, sound, they	11	mood
11	often	13	feelings
12	about, and, are, for, hard, life, times	14	banjos, guitars
13	ideas, use, words	15	artists, harmonica
14	on, was	16	friends
15	play	17	band, team
16	different, each, with	18	Chicago, festivals
17	be, learn, part, when	19	Chicago Blues Festival
18	at, Earth, has, together		
21	me, new, things		

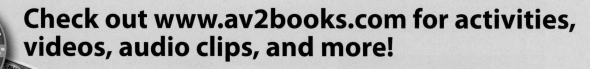